Piano Practice Games

- **Theory**
- **Technique**
- **Creativity**

Book 3

Authors
**Barbara Kreader,
Fred Kern, Phillip Keveren**

Consultants
Mona Rejino, Tony Caramia,
Bruce Berr, Richard Rejino

*Director,
Educational Keyboard Publications*
Margaret Otwell

Editor
Carol Klose

Illustrator
Fred Bell

CONTENTS

*✓

Students can check activities as they complete them.

ISBN 978-0-7935-6271-8

HAL•LEONARD®
CORPORATION
7777 W. BLUEMOUND RD. P.O. BOX 13819 MILWAUKEE, WI 53213

Visit Hal Leonard Online at
www.halleonard.com

Foreword

Piano Practice Games present imaginative ways to introduce pieces in **Piano Lessons** by coordinating technique, concepts, and creativity with the actual music in the lesson book. These preparation activities help focus learning by "playing with" each lesson piece aurally, visually, and physically.

Before each lesson piece is assigned:

Listen & Respond activities develop rhythmic and technical coordination.

active listening

Read & Discover activities reinforce understanding and recognition of musical patterns and symbols.

guided reading

After each lesson piece is mastered:

Imagine & Create activities expand knowledge of newly-learned concepts.

improvising and composing

Whether used in private or group lessons, **Piano Games** are all designed to make music. Many activities include accompaniments that can be added in the following ways:

Teacher

Audio CD

General MIDI Disk

May you enjoy many happy hours of musical discovery and success.

Best wishes,

Dakota Melody

(Lesson Book 3, pg. 5)

Feel the Beat!

As you listen to *Dakota Melody*:

1. Tap and count this rhythmic accompaniment. Remember to give the first note of every measure extra emphasis.

Tap throughout the piece.

2. Tap and count the rhythm of the melody. Add dynamics for a special effect.

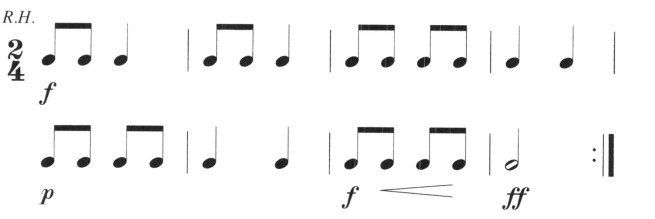

Extra for Experts!

Add a musical accompaniment to *Dakota Melody* by playing **E** in the R.H. and **A** in the L.H. in the following rhythm:

Play one octave lower.

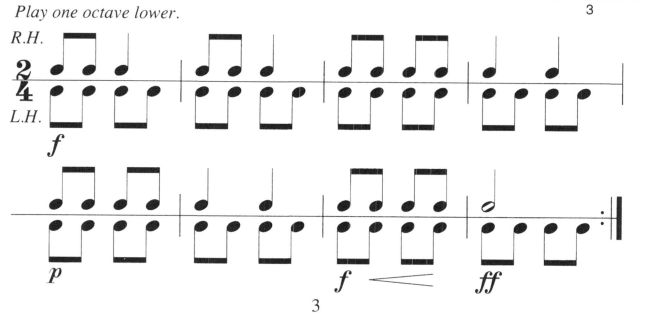

Hiccups in School

(Lesson Book 3, pg. 6)

Reading Warm-up

As you listen to *Hiccups In School*, add a musical accompaniment by playing the following warm-up:

Note: As a duet, the teacher plays "Hiccups In School" with L.H. as written and R.H. 8va lower.

Read & Discover

Map it out!
by Rebecca Shockley

To create a map of *Hiccups In School,* place a piece of tracing paper over the lesson book score.

1. Write "R.H." above each treble clef and "L.H." below each bass clef.

2. Draw a line connecting the noteheads in each hand.

3. Add the finger numbers for the beginning R.H. and L.H. notes in each measure.

For example, measures 1-3 of your map will look something like this:

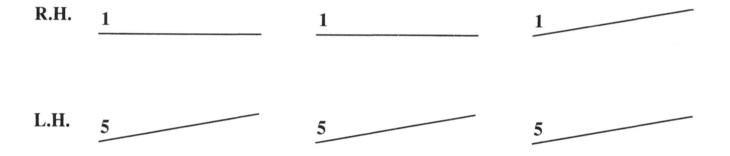

R.H.   1   1   1

L.H.   5   5   5

Search and Find

Using your lesson book as a guide, write the answers in the boxes below.

1. Which hand begins every measure?

2. How many measures have repeated notes in the R.H.?

3. How many measures have repeated notes in the L.H.?

Little Bird

(Lesson Book 3, pg. 7)

As you listen to *Little Bird*, tap and count the following rhythm:

Tap throughout the piece.

Read & Discover

Reading Warm-up

1. Using your lesson book as a guide, write the finger numbers in the blanks above or below each note.

2. As you listen to the accompaniment to *Little Bird*, play the following warm-up.

Allegro

mf

Note: As a duet, the teacher plays this accompaniment:

Allegro

Play 4 times | *Last time*

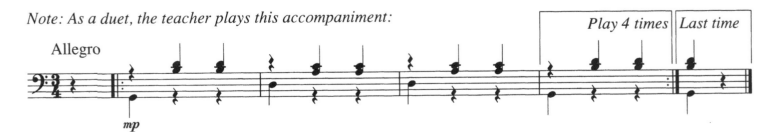

mp

Shortbread Boogie

(Lesson Book 3, pg. 9)

Be your own arranger!

When you experiment with a piece by playing it in a different way, you are playing a **variation.**

Changes in the melody create <u>melodic variations</u>; changes in the accompaniment create <u>harmonic variations</u>.

Playing Melodic Variations

1. As you listen to the accompaniment, play the melody to *Shortbread Boogie.*

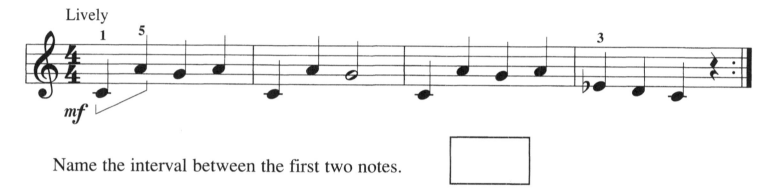

Name the interval between the first two notes.

2. Change the second note in every measure to **G** by writing it in the shaded box below. Play this **melodic variation.**

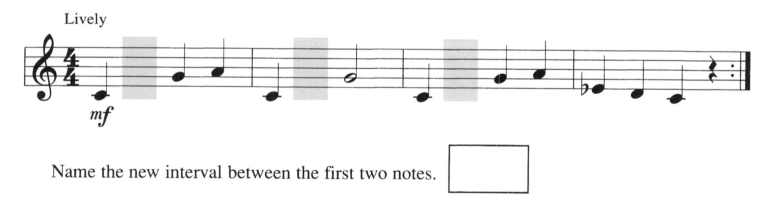

Name the new interval between the first two notes.

Playing Harmonic Variations

As you listen to *Shortbread Boogie*, play each of these variations of the L.H. accompaniment.

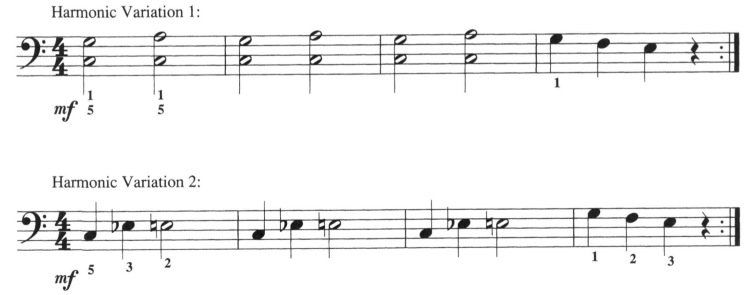

Harmonic Variation 1:

Harmonic Variation 2:

Note: As a duet, the teacher plays the R.H. melody of "Shortbread Boogie."

Combining the Melody with the Harmonic Variations.

As you listen to the accompaniment, play *Shortbread Boogie* in three different variations.

Melody with Harmonic Variation 1:

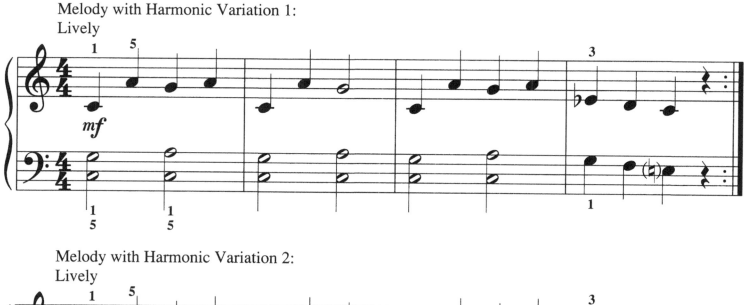

Melody with Harmonic Variation 2:

Extra for Experts!

Using the melodic variation you wrote out on page 7, play *Shortbread Boogie* again using Harmonic Variation 1.

Lavender Mood

(Lesson Book 3, pg. 10)

In *Lavender Mood,* the melody of every phrase begins the same, but ends differently. Using your lesson book as a guide, complete the phrases below by writing in the missing notes.

L.H. plays the melody.

Imagine & Create

Create your own piece!

As you listen to the accompaniment of *Lavender Mood,* use the six keys pictured below to improvise your own piece with your R.H.

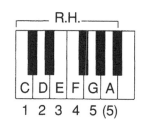

Now change the mood!

As your teacher plays the jazz waltz accompaniment below, use the same notes you played above to create a different piece.

Accompaniment (Student plays two octaves above Middle C.)

Take Me Out To The Ball Game

(Lesson Book 3, pg. 14)

Read & Discover

Reading Warm-up

As you listen to the accompaniment to *Take Me Out To The Ball Game*, play this *fill-in melody*, which makes a story of its own. Remember to count the measures of rest.

With energy

Play one octave higher than written.

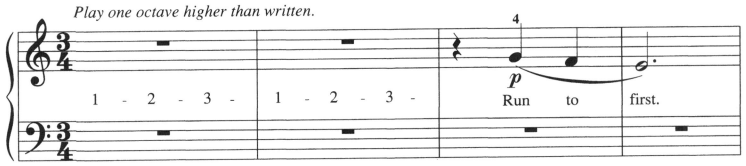

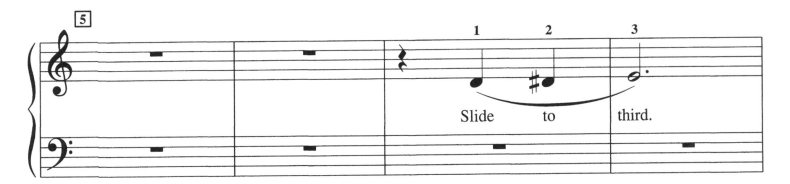

Bring me home.

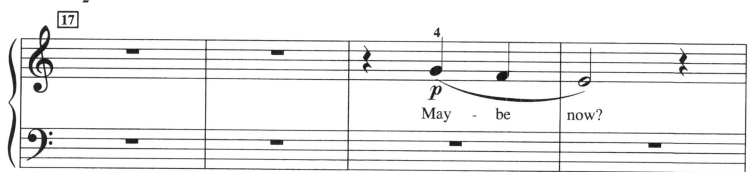

May - be now?

Oh! No!

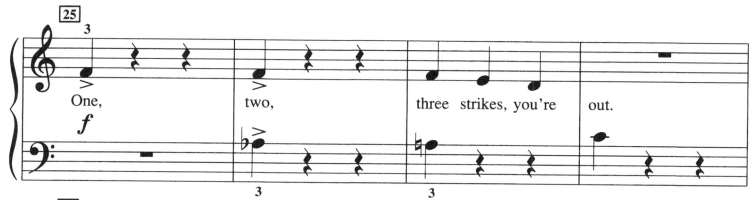

One, two, three strikes, you're out.

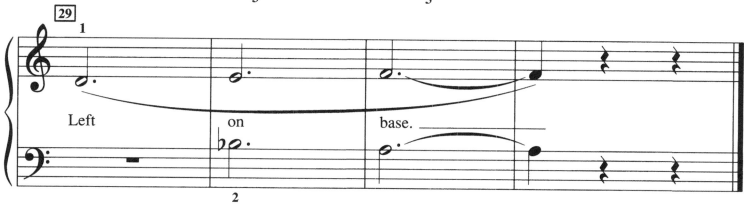

Left on base.

13

Spring

(Lesson Book 3, pg. 17)

The theme from *Spring* is one part of a longer work for orchestra called *The Four Seasons*. It was written by the Italian Baroque composer Antonio Vivaldi (1678-1741).

Listen to *Spring* three different times, tapping and counting the following rhythms throughout the piece:

Read & Discover

Reading Warm-ups

This warm-up will help you learn *Spring* more easily.

1. Using your lesson book as a guide, write the finger numbers in the blanks above or below each note.

2. As you listen to *Spring*, practice this warm-up until you can play it easily.

Note: As a duet, the teacher plays the R.H. melody of "Spring" 8va higher.

3. Open your lesson book to *Spring*. Write a new warm-up by completing measures 5-6 followed by measures 11-12 on the staff below.

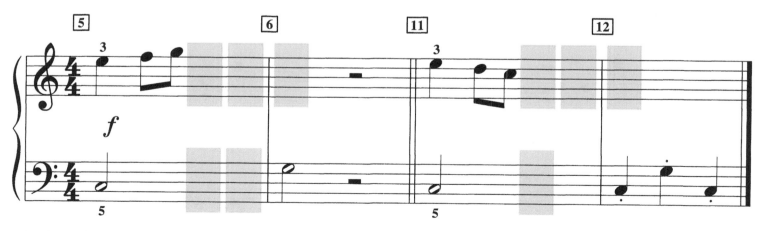

4. Practice this warm-up until you can play it easily.

Bounces

(Lesson Book 3, pg. 18)

Finger Taps

As you listen to *Bounces*, tap and count
the rhythm below using the fingers indicated.

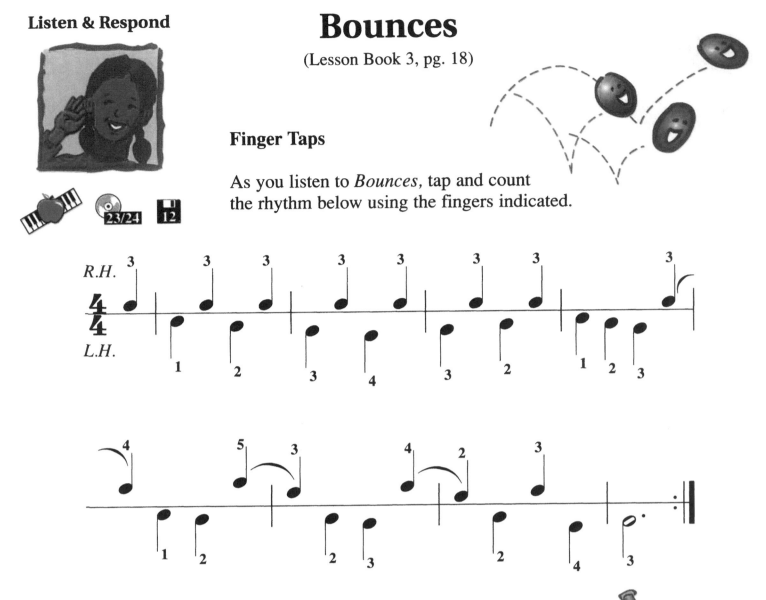

Read & Discover

Add a bassoon part!

The **bassoon** is a member of the woodwind
family of instruments. It plays in the bass clef
and has a deep, nasal sound.

As you listen to *Bounces*, read and play the
bassoon part written below:

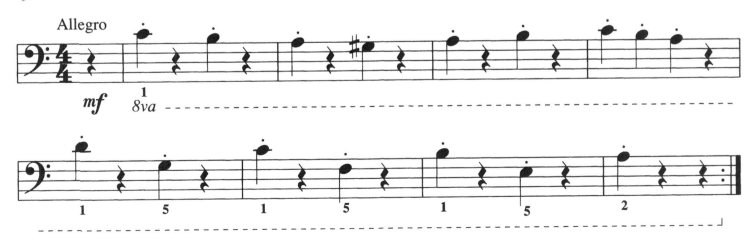

All Through The Night

(Lesson Book 3, pg. 19)

Keep the pulse!

As you listen to *All Through The Night*, tap and count the following rhythm:

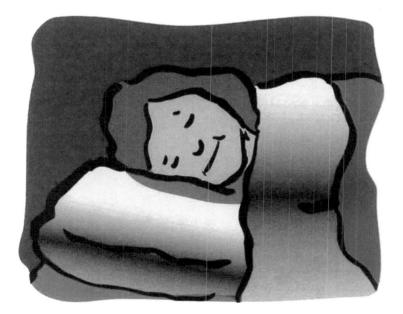

17

Dixieland Jam

(Lesson Book 3, pg. 22)

Listen to *Dixieland Jam* three different times, tapping and counting the following rhythms throughout the piece:

Imagine & Create

Inchworm Waltz

(Lesson Book 3, pg. 23)

Play *Inchworm Waltz* as a duet!

A piano *duet* is a piece for two pianists at one keyboard.
It is written in two parts:
   primo (the upper part) and
   secondo (the lower part)

To make *Inchworm Waltz* into a duet, play the **primo** part from the lesson book one octave higher than written. Play the **secondo** part below one octave lower than written.

Secondo

Moderately, with humor

19

Read & Discover

Setting Sun

(Lesson Book 3, pg. 24)

Technique Tunes
by Katherine Glaser

The *Setting Sun* hand position is made up of **whole steps**. Each hand plays a group of whole steps called a **whole-tone pattern**.

As you listen to the accompaniment to *Setting Sun*, play the **Technique Tune** below. Play each whole-tone pattern (𝅘𝅥𝅮𝅘𝅥𝅮𝅘𝅥𝅮𝅘𝅥𝅮) with one impulse of the arm and hand, paying close attention to the dynamic markings.

These small boxes are called "clusters."
Play notes together using the fingers indicated.

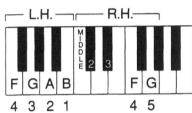

— *Hold pedal down throughout.*

Note: As a duet, the teacher plays this accompaniment two octaves higher than written:

20

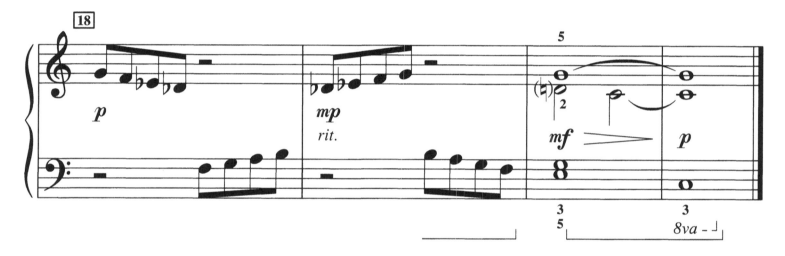

Imagine & Create

Get ready to create your own Impressionistic piece!

Impressionist composers such as Claude Debussy (1862-1918) and Maurice Ravel (1857-1937) tried to capture moods and pictures in sound. Whole-tone patterns and lots of pedal are two of the "tools" composers used to create these musical pictures.

Using the two whole-tone patterns you played in the **Technique Tune** above, improvise your own piece borrowing one of Debussy's titles:

The Sunken Cathedral
The Snow Is Dancing
Fireworks

Experiment with these whole-tone sounds all over the keyboard using the damper pedal.

Quadrille

(Lesson Book 3, pg. 28)

Reading Warm-ups

The *Quadrille*, an 18th-century French square dance, was also the name of a popular card game. Joseph Haydn (1732-1809), a composer during the Classical Period, probably danced and played the *Quadrille*.

1. Play this outline of the R.H. melody.

Repeat as necessary

2. Play this outline of the L.H. accompaniment by holding the blocked chords.

Repeat as necessary

3. As you listen to *Quadrille*, play the following reading warm-up.

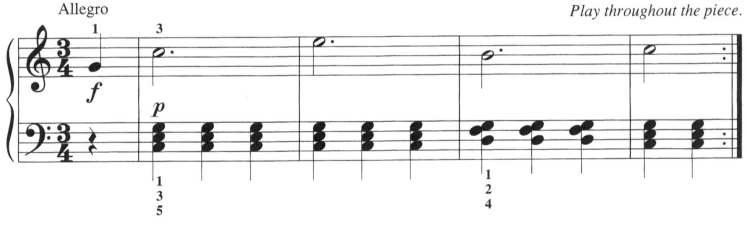

Extra For Experts!

Vary the L.H. accompaniment by playing it in broken chords as shown.

Note: As a duet, the teacher plays the melody of "Quadrille" 8va higher.

Scherzo

(Lesson Book 3, pg. 30)

Reading Warm-up

The following warm-up assigns the sound of the *flute* to the right hand and the sound of the *cello* to the left hand.

1. Using your lesson book as a guide, write the finger numbers in the blanks above and below each note.

2. As you listen to the accompaniment to *Scherzo*, imagine you are part of the orchestra by playing the following warm-up.

Allegro
Play R.H. one octave higher throughout.

Note: When played with teacher accompaniment, student plays both hands 8va higher throughout.

The Fife 'n' Horn

(Lesson Book 3, pg. 33)

Listen & Respond

Feel the Beat!

As you listen to *The Fife 'n' Horn*, tap and count the following rhythm:

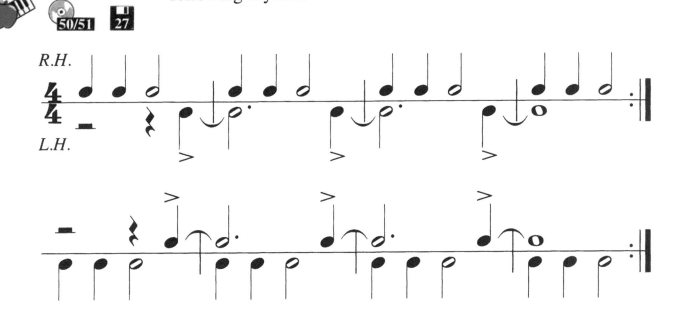

Read & Discover

Reading Warm-up

Before you play *The Fife 'n' Horn* from your lesson book, practice the following warm-up. Hold the accented notes with one hand while playing *staccato* with the other hand.

This warm-up feels like a "tongue twister" for your hands and fingers!

Imagine & Create

Join the orchestra!

The **fife**, a little flute with open holes, first appeared as a military instrument during the Middle Ages. It was the fifer's duty to play while the soldiers marched.

As you listen to *The Fife 'n' Horn*, read and play the following piece, imagining the sounds of the harpsichord, fife and horn.

Note: As a duet, the teacher plays "Fife 'n' Horn" 8va higher and the student plays the warm-up 8va lower.

25

Chorale

(Lesson Book 3, pg. 34)

A "chorale" is a hymn tune, a sacred melody.
Open your lesson book to the score of *Chorale*.
This *Chorale* includes parts for high voice,
middle voice and lower voice.

As you listen to the music, trace the phrases with your finger.
Lift your wrist at the end of each phrase.

Notice how the melody passes from the high voice to the low voice.

Read & Discover

Let's go on a Measure Hunt!

Using your lesson book as a guide, answer the following questions:

1. How many times does each example appear in *Chorale*?
    Write the number in the box next to each example.

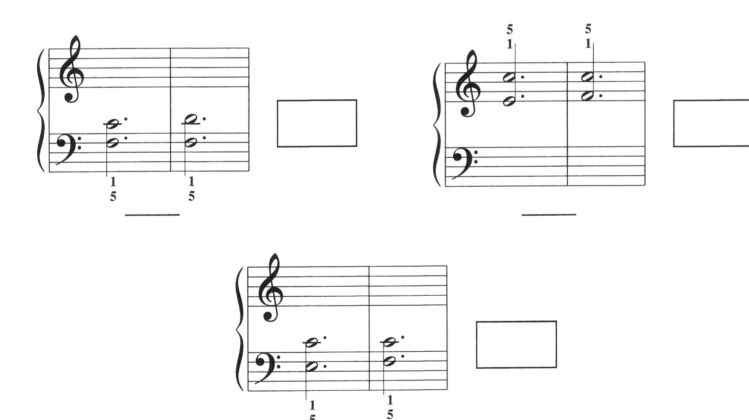

2. A pitch that repeats in the same voice is called a **common tone**.
    Write the name of the common tone in the blank below each example above.

3. Play each example until you can move smoothly from one interval to the next.

Reading Warm-up

1. Using your lesson book as a guide, write the R.H. and L.H. finger numbers in the blanks below.

2. Play the following warm-up.

Slowly

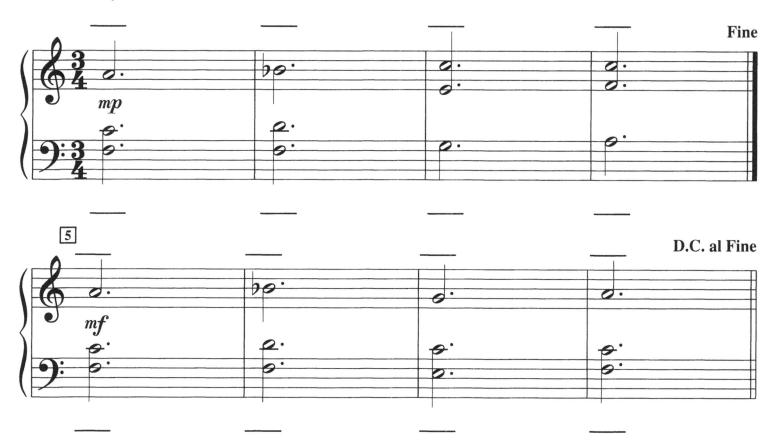

Note: As a duet, the teacher plays "Chorale" as written, and the student plays the warm-up two octaves higher.

Imagine & Create

Add a Descant!

In a chorus, the soprano voices sometimes add a part higher than the melody called a <u>descant</u>. As you listen to *Chorale*, improvise your own descant using the five notes pictured below.

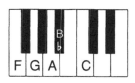

Walk Around The Block

(Lesson Book 3, pg. 35)

Technique Tunes
by Katherine Glaser

1. Complete the missing five-finger patterns in the empty measures, using the same rhythm as measures 1 and 2.

2. Write the name of each pattern in the blanks below.
   The first two are already done for you.

3. As you listen to *Walk Around The Block*, play *Five-Finger Swing*.
   Remember, in swing rhythm, eighth notes are played unevenly.

Five-Finger Swing

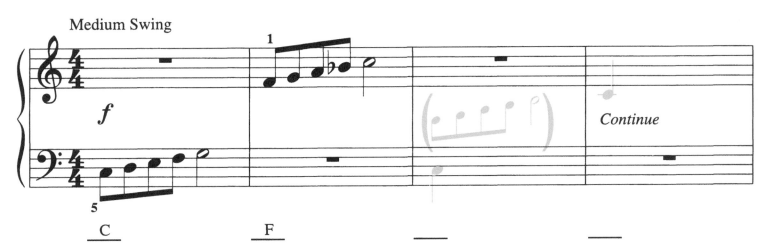

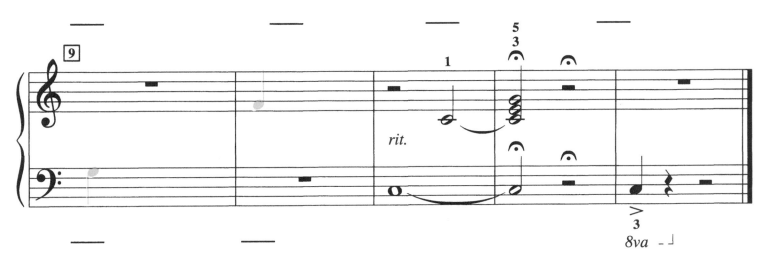

Note: As a duet, the teacher plays "Walk Around The Block" 8va lower and the student plays "Five-Finger Swing" 8va higher.

Romance

(Lesson Book 3, pg. 38)

Romance uses the **a minor 5-finger pattern**.

1. With your pencil, fill in the root (R), third (3rd) and fifth (5th) notes in the R.H. pattern below.

2. Fill in the second (2nd), fourth (4th) and fifth (5th) notes in the R.H. pattern below.

Now you can play the teacher's part!

Prepare to play the teacher accompaniment for the last eight measures of *Romance*.

1. Practice the chord warm-up below.

2. Name each R.H. note by writing
   R, 2, 3, 4 or 5 in the blanks.

3. Read and play the accompaniment below.

Imagine & Create

Get ready to improvise!

1. Ask your teacher to improvise in the **a minor five-finger pattern** as you play the accompaniment above.

2. Trade parts.

Fierce Heart

(Lesson Book 3, pg. 41)

Feel the rest!

You can make a drum sound by using an empty box and two wooden spoons to play the following rhythm activities.

1. As you listen to *Fierce Heart* play the drum *on the quarter rest.*

Play throughout the piece.

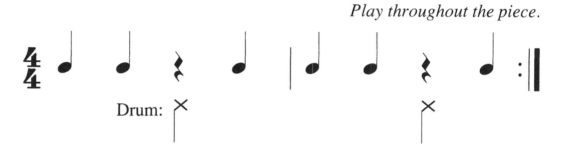

2. Listen again to *Fierce Heart*, and tap and count the following rhythm:

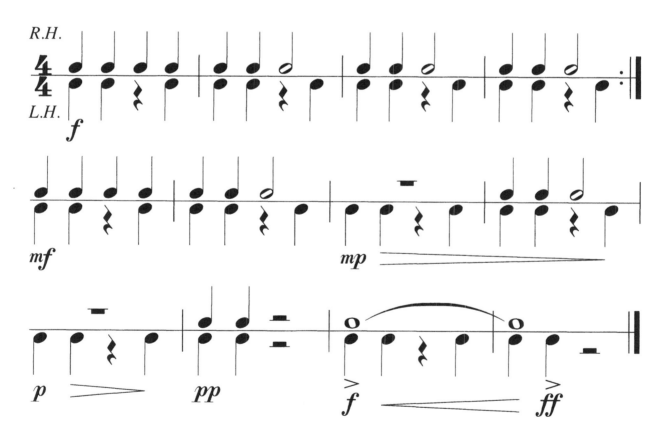

Read & Discover

Reading Warm-up

1. As you listen to *Fierce Heart*, play the tenor part below.

2. Using your lesson book as a guide, copy the bass note below the tenor part by adding it in each measure.

3. As you listen to *Fierce Heart* again, play the tenor and bass parts.

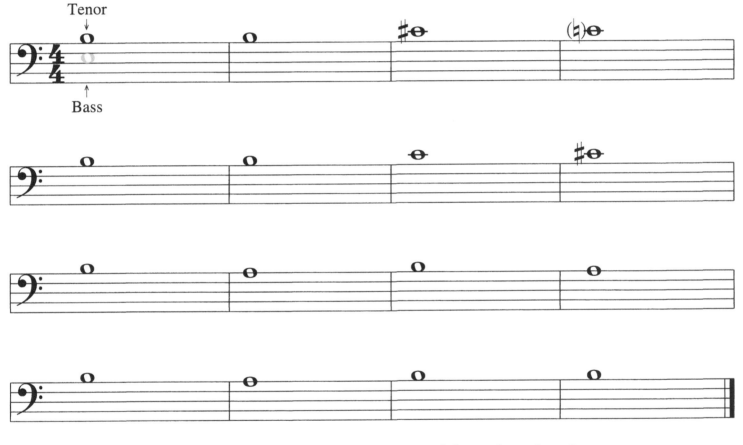

Note: As a duet, the teacher plays "Fierce Heart" 8va lower and the student plays the warm-up 8va higher.

Medieval Muse

(Lesson Book 3, pg. 43)

Get ready to improvise!

1. Practice this L.H. ostinato found in *Medieval Muse*.

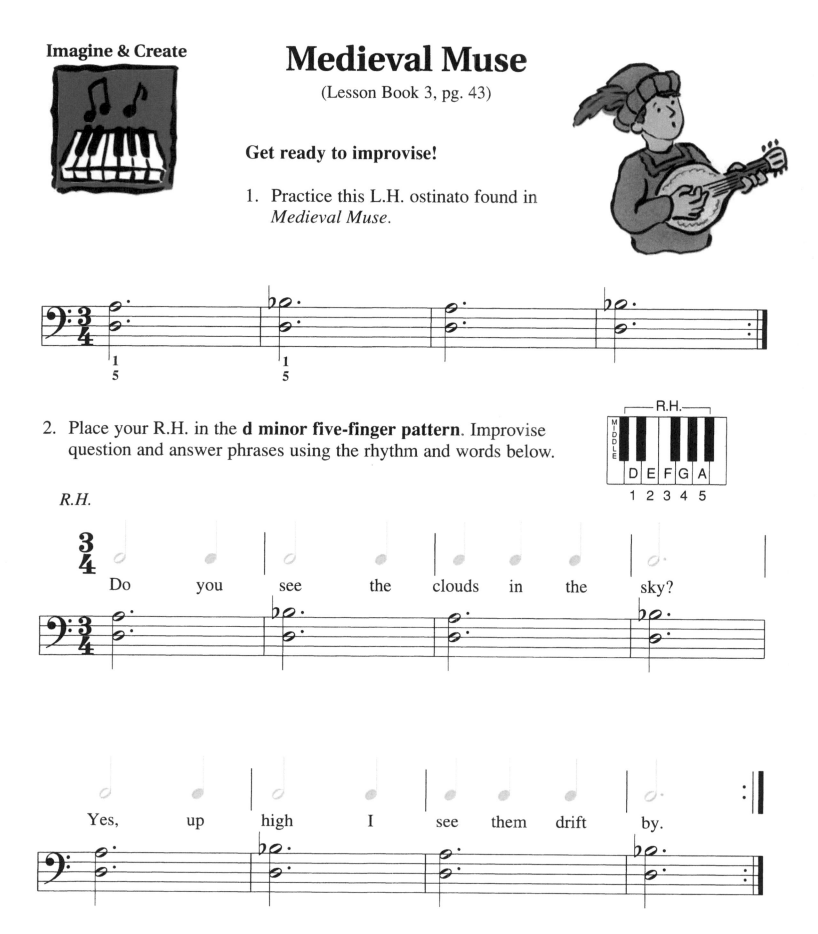

2. Place your R.H. in the **d minor five-finger pattern**. Improvise question and answer phrases using the rhythm and words below.

R.H.

Do you see the clouds in the sky?

Yes, up high I see them drift by.

3. Improvise hands together by playing the L.H. ostinato as you create new questions and answers in the R.H. part.

Floating

(Lesson Book 3, pg. 44)

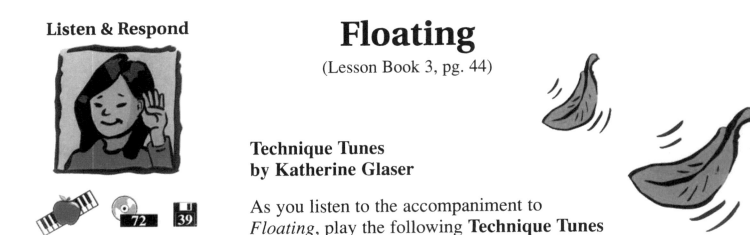

**Technique Tunes
by Katherine Glaser**

As you listen to the accompaniment to *Floating*, play the following **Technique Tunes** one octave higher than written.

1. Blocked chords

Very slowly

Continue the two-measure patterns, moving down until you reach **C.**

2. Broken chords

Very slowly

Continue the two-measure patterns, moving down until you reach **C.**

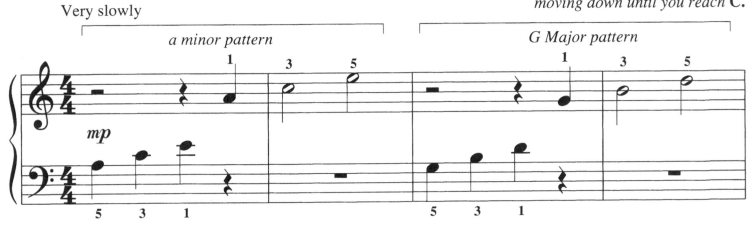

Imagine & Create

Get ready to improvise!

As you listen to the accompaniment to *Floating*, play this L.H. ostinato. It uses the Root (R) and fifth (5th) tones of each five-finger pattern.

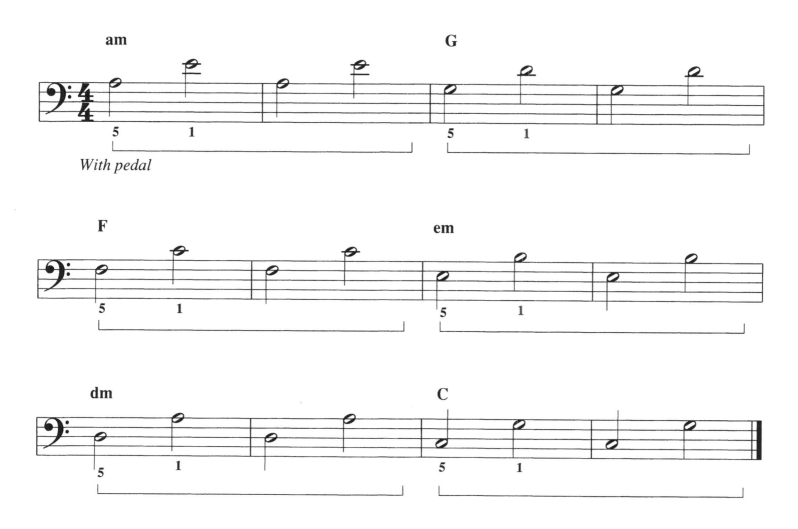

2. While you play this ostinato, improvise a R.H. melody. Use the notes in the five-finger pattern that match each L.H. position.

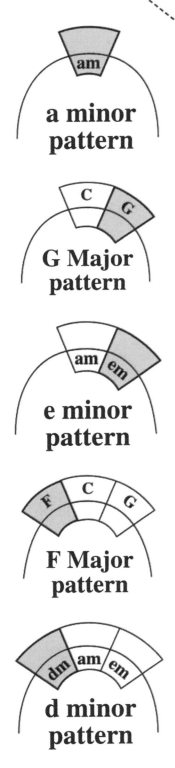

Five-Finger Matching Game

1. Draw lines matching the pattern names to the correct keyboard diagrams.
2. In the circles, write the letter names of the tones of each five-finger pattern.
3. With your pencil, fill in the circles that identify the Root, 3rd, and 5th.

C Major pattern

a minor pattern

G Major pattern

e minor pattern

F Major pattern

d minor pattern

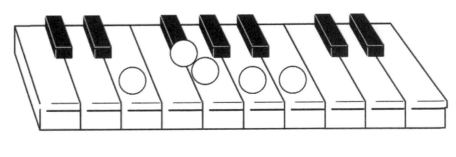

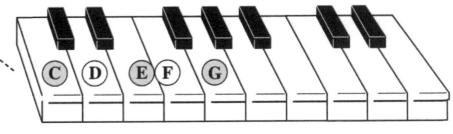

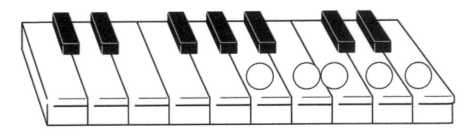

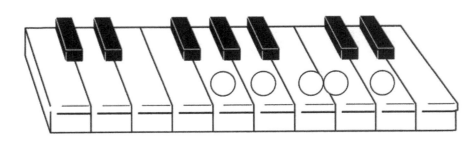

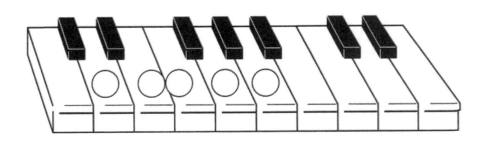

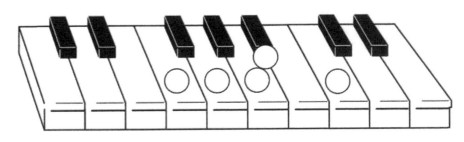

Read & Discover

Joy

(Lesson Book 3, pg. 45)

Reading Warm-up

As you listen to *Joy*, play these warm-ups one octave higher than written.

1. Play with the R.H. thumb only.

2. Add the fifth (5th) tone above each root (R) with your fifth finger.

3. Complete the triads by adding the third tone (3rd) above each root (R) with your third finger.

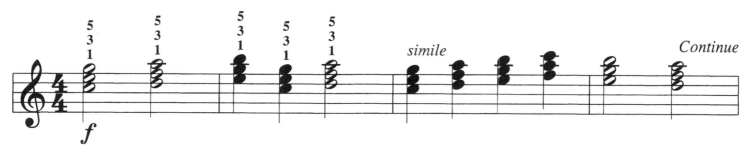

Note: As a duet, the teacher plays only the L.H. of "Joy" as the student plays each warm-up.

Read & Discover

Fresh Start

(Lesson Book 3, pg. 46)

Reading Warm-up

As you listen to *Fresh Start*, play this warm-up:

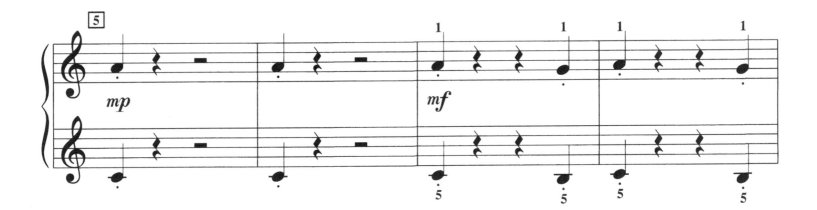

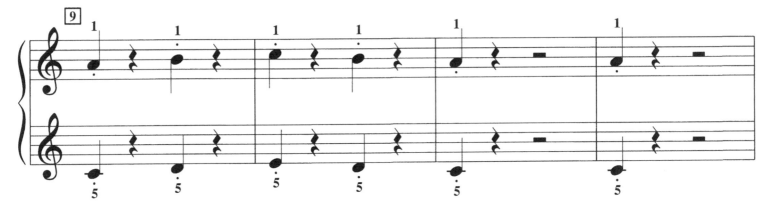

Note: As a duet, the teacher plays "Fresh Start" 8va lower and the student plays the warm-up 8va higher.

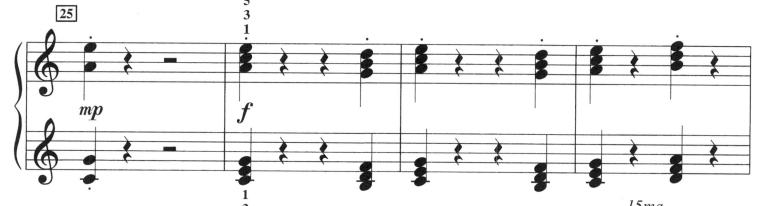

Playing Major and Minor Pairs

Drifting Clouds uses three related pairs of major and minor broken chord patterns:

C Major - a minor   F Major - d minor   G major - e minor

1. Imitate the sound of a harp as you play this piece.

Drifting Clouds

2. Improvise your own piece by playing the same triads from top to bottom or in any other way you can imagine.